Copyright © Shana Marlayna Chow.

All rights reserved. No part of this publication may be reproduced, distributed, or transmitted in any form or by any means, including photocopying, recording, or other electronic or mechanical methods, without the prior written permission of the author, except in the case of brief quotations embodied in critical reviews and other noncommercial uses permitted by copyright law.

ISBN: 978-1-09622349-8 (Paperback)

First Edition, August 2019.

All works written by Shana Marlayna Chow.
Edited and book design by Johnny Hamilton.
Cover photography by Marja Chow; image editing by Chantal Stermer.

www.shanachow.com

*To anyone going through the unrelenting pain of a heart break.*

# I Tried to Write Love Poems

Shana Marlayna Chow

# Table of Contents

Part 1: The Damage ..................................................3

Part 2: The "I-Hate-You-Miss-You-Resent-You" Complex..........45

Part 3: Miss Independent ..........................................95

Part 4: I Guess I Wrote Some Love Poems ...............................213

# Part 1
# The Damage

She went for a run outside today.
The first time she could put all
her weight on her foot *without pain*.
With each breath she breathed in the
fresh Spring air you get when the sun
rises but doesn't warm the grass yet.
She breathed in and out every
*name he called her*. Each bead of sweat,
it washed away *his scent*. As she ran
with her heart racing, the sun shined
on her skin and healed all her bruises
and cuts he made on her outside, but
so much more deeply on her insides.
And oh, did she get exhausted; and sadly
so programmed that to think maybe
she should *run back*. But she envisioned
an imaginary finish line. Though when she
crossed it, there were no crowd cheering,
hands raised, it was just her,
out of breath, out of the shell of a
person she became. She didn't raise
her hands to cheer, she didn't smile
because smiling was something that
was hard for her to do recently,
but she,
went for a run *outside* today.

And on a beautiful gold platter
you placed your demons in front of me,
and let them attack.

The devil was just sleeping,
see - he was there all along,
just resting to a lullaby
resting to his favourite song.
But month-by-month he awoke,
and slowly started to say,
"Give me your soul,
I own you, I control today."
Walking on eggshells
that started to slice her feet,
the pain became normal
as she did whatever he pleased.
But then one night she saw it,
the devil in full force,
fire in his angry mouth,
as he burnt her with his torch.
As he fell asleep tired
with whiskey on his breath,
she ran away in darkness,
with tears, fear and regret.
He found her in a cave,

starving, weak, and ill,
promised he'd be different,
promised he'd stop taking pills.
She went back to him so fragile,
didn't know where to turn,
and when anger returned again
he forced against her will.
And as she lay there vacant,
as he pounded her she cried,
she knew within that moment,
if she stayed there,
she'd die inside.
So she pre-planned her escape,
and never looked back,
except when people tell her,
that he's doing great and intact.
She doesn't care about image,
or what he posts online,
because against the fake smiles,
she will always see the true devil inside.

Turns out
you became the person
*you said you would never be.*
Turns out
I became the sucker who
*actually believed you.*

Where were you?
When all the sadness
overflowed and
I almost drowned...
Where were you?
When all your dirty
footprints refused
to wash away...
Where were you?
When my body still
had your fingerprints,
no matter how many times
I took soap to my skin...
Where were you?
when my white sheets,
refused to let go of
your scent...
Where were you?
...you were simply,
just
with
*her.*

For what it's worth,
I'll always know
your beginning with her,
overlapped with
you pleading
not to let us end -
and that is satisfaction in itself.

Don't hate the girl he cheated on you with,
he was feeding her the exact same bullshit
he was feeding you.

She had *no fight* left in her.
Not that she wasn't a fighter,
*she would always be a fighter.*
She just had *no fight* left in her
*for him.*

She felt as if there wasn't one part of her soul
that he didn't take from her,
but in this moment,
she realized,
he never took away,
*her strength to leave.*

I use to imagine our wedding day,
a vision on top of a mountain
the clear light blue Mediterranean Sea in the background.
The wind swaying my dress lightly and my hair
blowing as I had tears of pure happiness.
I would look at your face smiling back and we
would both share that moment.
But the years went on,
your true self was revealed
and the hurt started.
This vision slowly became blurred.
Like someone spilled water on a half dried painting,
a censored image on television,
your face became distorted.
I could no longer see your smile,
*that was the first to go.*
Your face wasn't there
but your body remained.
The more *names* you called me, the more your
strong arms that once protected me, hurt me, the more they *blurred out too.*
Pastel colours coming together,
until all you are is a blurry man,
and I see myself standing on that mountain
in a white dress trying to see your face again.
No tears of happiness, just tears of pain.
I closed my eyes to escape, and when I opened them,
you were gone. Completely.
And as I sit here and think of all you have done,
I can still find it in me to hope you find your peace one day.
Because I have no option but to find peace now.
So now, when I close my eyes and
envision myself, standing in that dress,
hair blowing in the wind,
a man who deserves me,
stands across from me
the smile is clear,
though his face is blurred.
It won't be blurred for long.

*I Tried to Write Love Poems*

I am numb
I am dumb
I took you back
and you did it
*once again.*
Shame on me,
for never being able to see,
how you got me
to believe
that I could never succeed
without you,
towering over me.
Your drug addiction
made an affliction
on my soul
I'll always know
that you are sick
so take your pick
of what evil
you want to depict.
Now I am free
so let me be
free from the damage
you have caused me.

I reached my hand all the way to the back of my head
and found a zipper.
I slowly pulled, and my skin started to move,
inch by inch, opening up like I was unzipping a
winter jacket. The sounds of the old layer
falling from my body was a sound I had never heard before.
Raw. Free. Fearful. But oh, how I just wanted to feel something,
as numbness was all I was used to. Anger.
*Embarrassment of being so naïve.*
As the zipper pulled down my face, my chest, my belly, all the places
sacred, I got to my feet and let the old layer of skin drop to the floor.
Like a child getting out of a snowsuit, I took one-step, and then another.
I stood there naked.
I stood there alone. Free. Raw. Pure.
Ready to begin again.

He found out
she is getting
a new last name.
That she finally
moved on, that
she is engaged.
He thought he was
over her, but
he made the
wrong choice.
Loneliness is all
he hears instead
of her voice.
He left her in tears,
all alone that night
in the pouring rain.
Thought he'd be
better off without her,
and she'd be the same.
But today it hit him
hard, there's no one
left to blame.
Yes, she will be getting,
a new last name.

If you asked
her to name
the best skill he has,
she would say
he was best
at making her feel like she
was the *only one*
when
*she wasn't.*

He was manipulation, at its finest.

At the end of the day,
you can't put a filter
over an ugly heart.

His life with her is no more *perfect* than it was with you,
he doesn't change,
his story does.

She left that love, and escaped her own suicide.

He was *everything* she wanted in a man: he was *everything* wrong for a woman.

We all *mistake love*.
we mistake it for money,
we mistake it for compliments,
we mistake it for kisses on necks,
and bare skin on bed sheets.

We all *blame love*,
we blame it for our stupidity,
we blame it for our trust issues,
we blame it for our pain.

But maybe instead,
we should look within ourselves,
for not learning love proper,
for not taking the time to understand,
and for not *loving ourselves enough to try.*

And maybe, they were just
addicted to each other's craziness.

He mended hearts with class,
and broke them with charisma.

Take me back to the blue sky
Take me back to the breeze
Take me back to the moment
when everything was at peace

Take me back to starlight
Take me back to no cares
Take me back to giggles
with no thoughts of despair

Take me to when we first met
Take me to when I didn't know
Take me to the first eye-lock
when you took my hand to go

Take me back to my senses
Take me back to my core
Give me the strength to let go
of always wanting more.

Inconsistency harbours distance -
attentiveness and presence creates love.

She's a firecracker
*trying* to light a fuse
in the middle of a rainstorm.

When someone apologizes so many times
about the *same thing*,
but continues to do
the *same thing*,
it's not sincerity,
it's wasted air.

For he wasted *too much* time, he should have claimed her, when she still *had* hope.

Never confuse *comfortable* with *love*.

If he truly loved her,
he would have wanted her to *conquer her dreams*;
and not coerce her to *conquer his*.

I think they got selfless love and selfish love confused.

You win,
you can have it all,
I'm taking back my *self-respect*,
and then I'll be on my merry way.

I wish I could say I haven't been here before,
but that would be a lie,
for these walls know all my demons
and the floors heard all my cries.

I wish I could say, I were *Wonder Woman*,
like I could throw cars above my head,
but this place knows all my mistakes,
this place knows where I've bled.

I wish I had a psychic to see the path to go,
but this place gently whispers in my ear,
"stay here where the sorrow flows,
stay here where the sorrow flows"

If I don't have a doormat outside my place,
why do you think I would be one for you?

Remember,
crazy people make for the best stories;
and damaged goods, are the best at being broken.

We all have both *tornadoes* and *sunshine* in all of us.
Surround yourself with those that bring out your *sunshine*.

What a mind trip you were.

He is not your Romeo,
and you are not his Juliet.
Pretty sure Romeo didn't
call Juliet a bitch,
and I'm sure as shit that Juliet didn't ball her eyes out
wondering if Romeo was going to
keep his dick in his pants.

Shana Marlayna Chow

It always amazes her how some men think with the
lower half of their body,
instead of their *brain*.

She lost *a bit*,
but *oh* how much of *herself* she gained back.

Part 2

# The "I-Hate-You-Miss-You-Resent-You" Complex

When did we become *too much*,
and when did we begin to care
*too little*.

Sweetheart,
was it closure
you wanted?
Or did you
really want
to leave
that door
unclosed?

Insecurities come in the cockiest of forms.

Amongst those cloudy days,
and stormy nights,
ice cold hearts,
and days apart.
Amongst it all,
through and through,
it was *always* you.
It was *always* you.

Here's to the *men* that value women with strong minds.

Don't be hard on yourself for giving time towards something that hurt you, because there once was a time when that was all you *ever wanted*. Respect your past decisions enough to value them as lessons on growth and prosperity, not harboured resentment. Let go, make peace with the past. Learn from it.

In life
some people can
verbally, mentally
and emotionally
*build you up.*
While others can verbally,
mentally and emotionally
*knock you down.*
Be smart enough to
know the difference.

The *healer* in me wants to believe you can change.
The *forgiver* in me wants to cheer for you.
The *optimist* may see a little light.
But the *realist* knows this is never going to work out.

They drink away their pain, and label it as having fun.

Never be the joker
in *his* deck of cards.

Maybe the reason why many of us are *lost in life* is because we can't say *no* without an explanation, and we can't explain *why* we say *yes*.

She'll bring you inspiration,
don't ever let her go;
she has poison on her lips,
and fire in her soul.

It's not love lost,
if you were *lost* the whole time
you were supposed to be *loving*.

She would have waited for him for eternity,
but he was already in line waiting for someone else.

*Everything* or *nothing*.
The one that makes your eyes light up,
your laugh turns hysterical,
and your hormones rise
in the right way.
*One and only*.
And if there is a second of slight doubt,
then please *just let me go*.
You'll hurt me now,
and *oh will it sting*,
if I can't be your everything,
I won't die being fragments of it.

You were the type of person
that I would be okay living in hell with.

Flowers don't heal bruises.

Don't be fooled by appearance,
if an angel sings the devil's words,
we all think it's a beautiful lullaby.

He said he didn't care. She believed him.

Accept the fact that you can't force anyone to change.
People walk to their own beats,
change to their own rhythms,
and on their own times.
If someone doesn't want change,
don't forget **you** always have a choice
to change *your* circumstances.

Give me the strength,
to grow my wings,
where I can fly like an angel,
away from these sins.
Where sunny warm beaches,
are all that's in sight,
where life isn't hard,
and I never sacrifice.

Because people who truly mean they're sorry
don't put a time limit on accepting their apology.

He said he cared,
that he was a *listener.*
*But silly girl,*
snakes don't have ears.

If you sweep your demons under the rug,
sooner or later you'll trip over the bumps.

It's not that she doesn't let people in,
she's just selective of who she gives her time to.
For she knows loyalty is hard to come by
in a world full of *crowd pleasers,*
and for that, when she loves, she loves with all her heart.

He never wanted to *learn how* to love,
he was a skilled pretender with deep pockets,
and a longing for attention.
And she,
she was naïve to the *idea of him*,
and had seen Cinderella one too many times.

The tears dripped down my face,
and quickly turned into *streams of chaos*.
But you took your handkerchief,
and with one single swipe,
made them disappear.
Until the next time
*you* create,
my *streams of chaos*.

The more years that go by and the older you get, you grow more wisdom. Your circle gets smaller, and things that used to get on your nerves trickle into small conversations. Misery loves company, and sooner or later you start to realize you don't like misery in your company. Family and loved ones come first, and you realize not all family are friends, and sometimes friends are closer than family. There comes a point where small things matter more. Where life is like trying to hold sand in your fist. The stronger you grasp your fingers into the sand, the faster it trickles through. You realize that life is for taking the time to cherish love, not rushing through to manifest regrets. As you get older, you realize love and well-spent time fuel your existence, and the other noises are chatter in the wind.

Life is too short
to be living someone else's.

And maybe in a different lifetime, we will meet again. The crazy will be gone. You'll be the man you once tried to be. I'll be the lady I should have always been to you.

*Sticks and stones*
do break my bones,
and *names* sometimes do hurt me,
but I'll smile as you attempt them both,
because those who cause pain,
tend to hurt the most.

Her poison was her fearless heart.

Even Wonder Woman needs a day off.

It wasn't the diamonds, or expensive bottles of champagne.
It was the time when she was nervous before an important meeting, where he would take a moment out of his busy day to stop her as she went out the front door and whisper in her ear, *"you got this."*
That is what made her *love him*.

But Sir,
you think shiny things and flashy objects will attract me,
but what you don't see,
is that your materiality only tempts the easily tempted.
So if all you have are items, *without any soul...*
well you have nothing that interests me.

Money won't make you classy.

Don't feed your *self-doubt*,
it's a hungry bitch,
that won't stop eating.

Sometimes giving up, gives more.

*Love* is rare.
I don't mean the superficial kind,
the type that exchanges *beauty for bank accounts*.
Or the settling kind,
the type that exchanges loneliness for mediocre boredom.
I mean real, passionate, to die for *love*.
That *love* is **rare**.

They say there will be a new moon tonight,
the stars will align where they should,
the forces will collaborate with your existence,
and in that very moment your world will change,
…but only if you look up and let it.

Let your mouth speak
what your heart feels,
give your raw soul
what it needs.

Sometimes I crave for imperfection
Sometimes all I want is perfect
At times I've hurt the *people I love*
At times the *people I love* have hurt me
But in this moment, all I want is the sound of
your heart beating against my bare chest,
while chaos no longer whispers in our ears.

A businessman walked through the green parkway with anxiety consuming his mind. Financial troubles, relationship issues, and lack of instantaneous success made him feel small. He felt sorry for himself as he sat down on a park bench, burying his face in his hands. He turned to his left and noticed a cheerful elderly man smiling at his surroundings, casually eating an English muffin.
"You seem rather happy," he stated to the old man.
The elderly man nodded, as he broke off a piece of his muffin and fed some pigeons "Sure am," he replied.
The businessman shrugged. "Well, why are you so happy?"
The old man turned to the businessman. "It's simple, I am happy to be alive…aren't you, young man?"
The businessman wasn't expecting that question. "Yes, I am. Of course."
The old man laughed to himself. "Sure doesn't seem like it."
The businessman knew his demeanor gave his mindset away. "Look, a lot of people have done me wrong. I am very stressed at the moment. What happened in your life to make you so damn happy?" He sarcastically asked the old man.
But the old man smiled back without insult. "I stopped blaming everyone for my circumstances."
"What do you mean?" The businessman asked.
The old man ate the last bite of his muffin, paused, and then turned to the man.
"It's simple, I wake up every day and live life. As people complained about circumstance, I decided to adapt. As people complained about the bad cards they were dealt. I took my cards, cut them in half, and stacked them on top of each other to get a better view. As people blamed their actions and reactions on others, I accepted my behaviors as my own. And instead of feeling sorry for myself, I felt love. You see, if you take too long trying to predict what is unpredictable, life will pass you by. You live in the moment, and be happy."
The businessman looked puzzled. "I don't blame anyone for my actions or reactions," he stated.

"You don't?" The old man asked.

The businessman thought for a moment and looked at a pigeon nearby. Suddenly he had an epiphany.

"Wait a minute... now I get what you meant. If you spend too long trying to predict the unpredictable... BUT no one can predict the unpredictable... because you can never predict it... it's a trick question... right?"

Wrapping his head around everything said, he turned his attention back toward the elderly man. But to the businessman's surprise, the elderly man was gone.

The businessman stood up, but the *wise old man with the answers to all life's questions* was gone. All that was left was a pile of crumbs that hungry pigeons continued to eat, and a businessman who just realized he wasn't living in this moment.

If anyone wants to change their life,
they have to want it from within.
Not want change to fix a mistake,
or regain notoriety they lost.
They have to have enough self-love
to change their layered soul.
Because if not for themselves,
all other reasons are plastic,
and plastic eventually melts
when it gets too hot,
and what good is melted plastic?

Their passion broke each other's hearts,
their love mended the pain –
their passion fixed each other's hearts,
their hearts were never the same.

Love a girl who holds you,
with flowers in her hair.
The one who wears white cotton,
and won't utter a single swear word.
Treat her like a princess and
make promises to keep.
Just don't make her
the same old ones,
that you never kept for me.

A soulmate is someone who you hand over
your whole entire heart to,
and if you separate,
it's the kind of love,
where when your
heart is given
back,
it *never*
comes back
the *same.*

# Part 3
# Miss Independent

*Your life* is a novel.
You can't turn back pages and dwell, or endlessly re-read what has already happened.
Nor can you skip a couple chapters, and bypass the painful and challenging parts.
Nor can you only read the good,
and exciting parts.
All you can do is live your life
the best you can, in this very moment.
Because this moment will never
be the same, and you won't get to have it again.
One month from now,
six months from now,
five years from now.
So keep flipping forward,
page by page.
Smile. Cry. Laugh.
Dog-ear the pages.
Trust the process.
Embrace your journey,
and *be kind to yourself.*

And over time,
the more names he called her
stopped chipping away at her,
but rather, they started to empower her,
because over time she realized they never changed -
but she did.

Insecurities speak loud and spiteful,
confidence dances in the silence of truth.

I want to stomp bare foot in a bucket of grapes to make wine.
I want to hike the Grand Canyon,
and take pictures jumping close to the edge.
I want to smile and magically form dimples on my cheeks because
my smile is too big.
I want to drive on the freeway, no GPS, no map, no destination,
just the summer air blowing through my hair.
I want to listen to intense Rocky theme music while partaking in
a water gun fight on the beach.
I want to see the world through new eyes.
I want to let go of all that was and all that has been.
I want to live.
Breathe.
Smile.
*I just want to be happy.*

One man's complaints, is another man's
*"how could he be so dumb to lose you?"*

If you try to understand why someone hurt you,
instead of reacting to the hurt,
you will be healed quicker,
than carrying that anger
in your soul.

BE COURAGEOUS.

little girl, little boy
life will fly by
and when you wake
upon the day,
you won't even
know why.

So breathe the air
and embrace the charms
of what this world can give,
and when you have
a choice to make,
always, be *courageous* within.

And the wise old monk said:
if you search for happiness in other people,
if you search for happiness in possessions,
if you search for happiness in money,
if you search for happiness in sex,
if you search for happiness in anything other
than first finding happiness within yourself, you will always be
*unhappy.*
Because people change, people leave,
things can break, and sex is just temporary pleasure.
Money comes, and money goes.
If you search for yourself in places you are not, you give the power
of your happiness away.
Control your happiness by finding it within yourself first.

-Judge Me-

You can look at pretty pictures,
and you can see pretty things,
you can look at a woman's body,
and think that's all she is.
But let me tell you something,
it's about her self-respect,
it's about her charisma,
it's about her intellect.
If you work hard for it, then own it,
because looks always fade,
educate your mind,
and to live freely every day.
So judge me for having confidence,
judge me for my tries,
judge me for my failures,
judge me for my lies,
judge me cause I'm giving,
judge me cause I'm naïve,
judge me for being insecure,
judge *me for being me.*
Looks are only superficial,
image is just a façade,
we are all human beings,
we are *all* inevitably flawed.
So smiles can change mornings,
and laughter can cure all pain,
and one day when you judge someone,
remember, it might be in the wrong way.

*Love your damn life.*
Do things you are afraid of.
Talk to random strangers.
Take pictures of *everything* and *anything*.
Skip down the street like a weirdo.
Run in the rain just for fun.
Tell people that you love them.
Dance even if your feet don't agree
with what you're making them do.
We all die – make your story a
motion picture, not a crappy commercial.
Don't waste it.
*Love your damn life.*

*Everything in moderation.*
You never hear a man on his death bed
say he wished he hadn't travelled the world,
or stay up all night to watch the sunrise.
Let loose, get what you need to out of your system.
Live life like you should, it will be gone before you know it.
And when the days get darker earlier, and that tan starts to fade,
rebuild, cleanse,
and crush some goals. *It's all about balance.*
Your life can be exactly what you want it to be.
Put in the work.
Focus.
See, failure – it's guaranteed.
Multiple failures – them too.
What isn't guaranteed is your ability to
push yourself back up, and keep going.
So make your determination *guaranteed.*
And when the days get lighter earlier,
and that tan starts to appear again,
embrace it.
*Everything in moderation.*

*Remember that mountain we built,*
with all the laughs, and jokes, and risk and trust, and smiles, and kisses on foreheads, and fights, and tears, and numbness and burnt egos. At times the mountain was big and strong, thought nothing or no one could tear it down. At times the mountain was weak, rocks rolling down, standing on the edge like it was about to crumble beneath our feet.
*Remember that mountain we built.*
Because I do. I remember how it all fell crashing down. I'll never forget how it slid and slopped and washed away all the good.
And when it settled, I stood at the bottom of the rubble. Broken.
But slowly, piece by piece, stone by stone, and every pebble in my fingertips, I started to build my own mountain.
And as I sit on top, I gaze in the distance, and realize how this view is nothing like I have ever seen before in my life.

You are art,
and art does not apologize
for being fierce,
fearless, or confident.

You almost never see it coming,
but sometimes
the best lessons
are the ones that shock you,
and the best motivations
come from the ones that hurt
you the most.

Never a victim.
Always a warrior.

As children, when we touch a hot surface and we get a burn, we learn not to touch it again. However, as adults, we get burns, and we have a tendency to go back. Regardless of the heat, regardless of the pain, regardless of the burn. But, the more we return back to what hurts us, the more burns we get, the deeper they go each time. The deeper the burn, the harder it is to heal. So be careful, burns turn into scars, and sure, scars can fade, but never disappear. So like a child, learn. Protect yourself from hot surfaces, and situations that hurt your soul.

Don't make your dreams framed in canvas.
Make your dreams a mural.

you will see the light
even if the moon
isn't shining bright
you aren't the wicked
names called
or the silence of
your past
you aren't regrets
buried
in what didn't last
you are sugar on
a tongue tip,
and dimples to
soft cheeks.
you are a giggle
among the sadness
and a loving body
on soft sheets
you are a hurricane
of giving
and autumn air
to refresh a face
you are a tyrant
to what you believe in
yes life is what you make
so lift your head up sweetheart
and tilt it back to laugh
stand up for yourself always
no you are not your past

Remember,
beautiful is never perfect -
and fairy tales
are boring.

everything suddenly changed
like and explosion
like and eruption
in an instant
all that was
was no longer
everything around her
was different
but like a sunrise
after a black night
she awoke
and when her
eyes opened
she was more herself
then she had ever
been before

She was born during
a full moon
when fearlessness circled
around the universe
and found its way
into her soul.

Our hearts are like a door.
We all start with the door wide open, but as the years go by, or relationships end, hurt, betrayal, and lack of trust manifest, that door starts to slowly close, inch by inch. We start to protect ourselves from pain. We leave the door half open, we start to fear the unknown, and are hesitant to let a stranger through the now small entrance. People can be so traumatized that the door gets shut completely, maybe even with a bolt in front. A form of *self-protection* through avoidance. But if you change your thoughts, the worst that can happen is you get your heart broken – and if you have made it through heartbreak once, you sure as hell can do it again. Love is worth the pain. So, be smart, don't leave your door wide open to be taken advantage of, but don't limit yourself from love and happiness by closing it shut. You deserve love.
You deserve to give love, be loved and feel loved.

*Forgiveness:* It isn't necessarily about a conversation, or a hug, or a hand shake.

It's not always about spoken words or resolutions. Sometimes it is having the courage to **forgive yourself.**

To *forgive yourself* for having an open and selfless heart when you shouldn't have.

To *forgive yourself* for letting naivety alter your judgement.

To forgive yourself for not being smart enough, strong enough, or wise enough, even though at the moment you thought you were.

To forgive *yourself enough* to learn, change and grow.

See, once you *forgive yourself,* that is when the real beauty erupts within you. The words will echo in your ear, saying *the past does not define you, your future is patiently waiting.* Believe me, in time, your heart will open again, and when it does, it will be like nothing you have ever felt before in *your life.*

That mountain only looks big
because you aren't climbing it.

To *be* angry and to *feel* anger
are two *separate* things.

When you *are* angry,
you act irrational,
you act on impulse,
you lose your filter,
and leave irreversible scars.

But when you *feel* anger,
you have control, which ultimately
leads to acceptance,
motivation,
and healing.

So instead, of *being* angry,
*feel* anger,
then open up the palm of
your hand, let that feeling sprinkle out
like dust, in the wind
and carry on with your
beautiful life.

**Sea breeze on her *face*
sunshine on her *skin*
peace in her *heart*
and new *memories*
to be made.**

And then she had a thought:
If she could make it through this,
if she just keeps on going,
she could make it
through anything.

It is only
in solitude
where you will grow, heal,
and gain the mental strength
to take on the life
that was always meant for you.

Just keep on going. This is your life.

I want to talk about philosophy,
and if you think there is life after death,
or the planets somehow align
while we are sleeping, or if dinosaurs were
actually alive when Jesus walked this earth
but were microscopic in size. I want to talk
about beliefs, and pick your brain full of the 7
wonders of the world, or the 7 wonders of your world.
I want to be intellectually stimulated.
Because you can be attracted to a body, you can be
attracted by a shape, but it's a mind that will always turn you on.

A lot can happen in
1 year;
5 years;
8 years;
10 years;
If you are going through a hard time,
think back to 10 years ago,
and how much you have accomplished.
All the hard days,
adversity you overcame.
All the accomplishments,
stresses, and never giving up.
10 years from now,
imagine what you could be.
Career, family, love,
*unconditional happiness.*
Life is a trip. Trip yourself out.

Don't dull your edges out, darling;
you'll never be what everyone
wants you to be,
and you shouldn't ever have to.

And above all
keep love in your heart,
the strongest people are fuelled by love,
not hate.

And to think –
Some of the most
important,
special,
and happiest days of our lives
haven't even happened yet.
Stay positive.

When you ask people about love,
so many of us will talk about pain,
we talk about the bad before the good,
we rarely talk about first glances
eyes locking, introductions, nervous laughter,
losing your train of thought, soft lips, kisses on cheeks, walking into objects, and the beginning. We lack conversations that talk of life partners,
never giving up, finding your soul mate, and fighting for your heart. In movies more than real life we see characters talk about holding a new born baby, smelling the soft skin and falling in love with the life you created. We so easily spend time talking about the pain more than the love. So instead, let's talk about love. Pain is inevitable, it is part of the process. Love is what makes your life make sense. Be open, be optimistic, be a hopeless romantic. Even if there is a little pain, the love is always worth it.

She is *dangerous*,
because she is peacefully insane
with absolutely no shame.
She isn't afraid to fail,
or fall on her face,
and watch as it crumbles,
beneath her feet.
One too many
*aces hidden up sleeves*,
washed away any trace
of her naivety,
and now chaos has
become entertainment,
a normalized task,
like her life is a game of
constantly rebuilding it,
and finding her peace,
to let slip and slide again,
then grow back into
her *golden throne*.
Yes,
*she is dangerous,*
*in all the right ways.*

We all get it confused,
we don't fear love,
we all *want* love.
What we fear is that the next person
will be like the last person
who played roulette with our hearts.
We all want love,
what we fear is *repetition*.

A woman sat on a sandy beach alone.
Hair blowing the salty air through her summer curls.
The sun was going down, and the summer air grew cooler by the minute.
Her knees were close to her chest as she wrapped her arms around them.
A couple spots over she noticed a handsome man sitting alone.
The light blue sky lit the man's olive coloured skin, and she could
feel his strong energy, but she could also feel his brokenness
like his sadness, pain and numbness were a cloud that followed him
around through the faint half smile on his face.
She decided to move closer to him.
The man noticed, but didn't move,
for the woman had a unique beauty about her.
At an arm's length away, she turned to him and asked,
"Name 10 things you love."
The man was taken aback by the randomness of the situation, but
recently had begun to feel rather alone; so he thought, *what the hell*.
The man began to name them: his dog, his parents, his friends,
his collector car… until he got to his 10th item. Once he finished,
before he could get another word out, the woman blatantly interrupted and said, "that's why you are broken."
The man started to think this lady was a little off her rocker.
"Excuse me?" He asked.
The woman replied, "I asked you to name 10 things you love."
The man understood and replied, "I did."
The woman smirked, "you never once named yourself."
The thought suddenly hit the man like a tidal wave.
She continued,
"If you don't love yourself,
you can't properly love anyone else…"
But, before the woman could finish her sentence the man interrupted,
"and this,
this is why I am so broken."

Shana Marlayna Chow

And even at your best,
a picture perfect person –
all your loose ends tied
in a pretty bow.
Even at your very best,
you will never be right
for the wrong person.

And remember, at your worst,
imperfect and full of mistakes,
loose ends frayed in multiple directions –
Even at your very worst,
you will always be right
for the right person.

And if I fly, I will fly
And if I slip, I will slip
And if I get lost, call me an explorer,
And if I find myself, call me a discoverer,
And if in the dark horizon,
I start to smile, instead of fearing the unknown,
my soul will be at peace,
as I will know,
this is the pathway meant for me.

And if you lose yourself amongst the reckless tides,
don't fight them –
get swept off into the unknown seas.

Sometimes you wonder where the *day went*,
other times you wonder where the *week went*,
be careful you don't wake up one day
and wonder where your *life went*.

The old man sat across from his grandson, on his panoramic patio that overlooked the Malibu coastline. Years of tribulations and successes were apparent on every wrinkle on his face. His eager Grandson asked,

"*Grandpa, what's the biggest mistake you ever made?*"

The old man folded his wrinkly hands together, and gave his grandson a slight smirk, then he calmly answered,

"*trying to please everyone.*"

It's so *easy* to be negative,
you'll never be disappointed if you fail,
because you risk absolutely nothing.
To be positive, is to be brave.
And to be brave is not *easy*.

She stood on the edge of the wooden dock
with her back to the water,
and her eyes closed.
She spread her arms wide, *like a bird,*
and she jumped back.
Water splashed on her silk skin,
the old layers swam away from her.
When she came up for air,
she took her first breath without a care in this world,
she took her first breath of her *new life.*

You're not meant to carry this world on your back.
Let that pain go.
Love more,
Laugh often,
and smile your heart out.

We are as *old* as the stories we tell,
and as *young* as our unconquered dreams.

She is *stardust* to her loved ones,
and a *no one* to this world.
But she'll keep pushing harder,
until she can't recognize the word *fear*.

I may not be where *I want to be*,
but damn...
I am a whole lot *closer*
than if I were to have
complained,
sat back,
and
*never tried.*

Her hair grew *8 inches that year.*
She travelled 8 out of the 12 months,
to deserted beaches and cobble stone streets.
Drank wine and followed it with cheesecake.
Went for scenic jogs in the sun, not hamster runs on the treadmill.
Hitch-hiked, took limousines, and rode bare back on horses.
She met people from all walks of life.
One with $800 to their name, one with $800 million.
She swam in oceans and lakes, met strangers and new friends.
And for the first time in her life *she felt free.*
Her hair grew *8 inches that year.*

Her eyes are beautiful,
not because of colour or shape,
but it's the *pain* they've seen,
and the *strength* they have
to continue peering out at this world
with never ending *hope*.

Don't let anyone make you feel insignificant.
Dream. Try. Conquer. Repeat.

Sad times make people either hardened, or strong.
You become so hardened by the hurt, that you self-destruct.
Or, you find strength in the vulnerability of the unknown,
and look onto the horizon like it is a kingdom waiting to be conquered.

Remember –
you are so much stronger than you think you are.

The more appreciation you give during your life,
the more you get back.

Whatever struggle you're facing,
whatever hardship feels never ending,
remember,
dark clouds *don't last forever.*
Time heals all,
and in turn, weaknesses dies,
and stronger mindsets survive.
And when those dark clouds finally pass,
you'll be a stronger person than you were before.

I want 50's music in my ears
and sunshine on my skin
I want a life full of happiness
and a never ending grin
I want lollipops and lakes
and never ending hope
I want to conquer this life
and all of the unknown.

*Believing in yourself* will get you a lot further than listening to people who gave up on their dreams.

Just. Be. Strong.

You have to live in the moment,
not live for the weekend,
not live for the perfect sunset,
or for the second when everything
*may* finally fall into place.
Because as you are *waiting,*
you are *wasting.*
You can't plan everything.
*Sporadic* is more
beautiful than *structure.*
Wear that outfit you've been saving,
tell your loved ones, that you *love them,*
and smile a little bigger today,
*especially* if times are hard.

The problem with broken people,
is that there is no problem,
we are all broken one way, or another.
What separates the survivors
are our reactions to pain.
Some grow strength from brokenness,
and some *don't*.

You can't continue to your full potential,
if you don't make peace with your past.
Even if it's in your own *mind*,
even if it's with only *yourself*.
Make that peace
to live the future *you* deserve.

It's never time *wasted*,
if your outlook *changes*.
You either *learn* and grow,
or *overcome* and still grow.

Remember,
your life doesn't have to be complicated,
every day you're given a new opportunity to change your mindset.

Show people you care.
You have nothing to lose,
only rejection for having
a kind heart.

there is a difference between being alone
and being lonely
it is acceptable
to not fear love,
to be open to it
yet still be content
being alone
it is a beautiful thing
to feel whole
yet still want to grow
there are no rules
or guidelines
you decide what
boxes you want to tick
and when you want
to tick them.

She's not *young*, but she isn't *old*.
She's not *rich*, but she ain't *poor*.
She's no *genius*, but she's not *dumb*.
She's got *obligations*, but not *limitations*.
She has a globe in her mind, spinning
and in this moment,
she realizes,
she can spin it,
and spin it,
and close her eyes.
And wherever
her finger lands,
she can go.

Who I was,
who I need to be;
I met my enemy,
and it was me.
No fear of rejection,
if it comes from myself.
Goodbye to who I was,
hello to my new self.

People say that
failure is *never* an *option*.

I don't believe that.

Failure *is* an option.

Failure knocks you down,
the one thing
that motivates you
to try even harder.

Don't live your life
as if you were dead
before you actually die.
Live the life
that was
always meant for you to live.

I will be a bull, and charge at my life.
Despite the steepness of the mountains,
or the blades of hail that shoot at my face,
I will continue.
Despite the thirsty blazing sun,
or words that leave the lips of new enemies
that burn my soul like daggers,
still, I will charge.
Despite losing loved ones, and the ache of a
broken heart, I will
still be a hopeless romantic.
I will continue. Until the last
breath that leaves my lungs,
I will be a bull, and charge at my life.

Of all the masks she's worn,
to make everyone else pleased,
she should have always known,
being herself is the best to be.

With glue,
thread,
tape,
and a little *old fashioned whiskey on the wound,*
she healed herself,
she rebuilt herself,
and her fear became a distant memory.

*You* can blame the Universe for your actions,
and *you* can place band-aids over *your* wounds.
But if *you* don't face your problems head on,
those band-aids start to wither and fall off.
Don't fall into the easy trap of *self-pity*,
and don't think yourself weak for admitting your flaws.
In the mirror, look, and be honest with yourself.
*Real change* only comes through truthful self-reflection.
Remember,
life is precious, *you* are precious.
Don't waste it.

She will not give into temptations that would alter her progress,
or believe the names yelled to her by fools,
she will not be dictated
by opinions of the overly opinionated,
nor the hate from those who hate themselves most.
She will stand when all odds are against her,
and smile when tears well in her eyes.
In this jungle she will be a lion,
and she will thank her disappointments
for making her rise.

The show must go on,
you must go on.

She'll teach you how to love her,
by loving herself first.
She'll teach you how to treat her,
by showing you her worth.
Love and respect are mutual,
if you care to understand.
Yes, she knows
you need a *Queen* to stand by you,
but she wants a *King*
to be her man.

You are not *your mistakes*. You are not all you have *done wrong*. When someone points out all your bad, and tries to define you using your errors, don't believe them. Weak people try to climb up by pulling down on the shoulders of others. Believe in your *strength*, you know who you are. You may know all your bad, but you *know* your good. Human beings make mistakes, and it's the weaker ones who knock you down, into the ditch to join them; and it's the stronger ones who continue encouraging you to overcome.

If you don't *motivate, encourage,* or *lift me up,*
then you have nothing for me.

And then the seasons changed back again,
Spring to Summer, Fall into Winter,
with her hoping, wishing, praying that everything
would be okay, that things would change for her.
That she would finally be at *peace* for once.
But this year was different, and once the ground beneath her
started to warm, her *peace* was no longer found in autumn leaves
of the Fall, or snowflakes of blizzards, or familiar surroundings
she thought would make everything ok. All along it was within
her own soul. It was just waiting, pulling and prying to manifest
from within. And when it did, she changed similarly to the seasons
dancing around her. Yes she changed, but unlike the seasons, she
*changed for good.*

She was trapped in a concrete cell.
Words of insecurity gnawed away at her already tampered ego, so she lived in her vacant, silenced mind; A place no one should ever live. One evening though, she saw a slender beam of light, through a tiny hole in the wall. She got down on her knees and used her nails to scrape away at the light in the stone. She continued to scrape away, bit by bit, piece by piece, until the hole was big enough. She put one leg through, then the next, until she could feel the cold air on her face. And for the first time in a long time, her voice was not silenced, her insecurity went hungry, her mind was no longer vacant. Her escape was complete -
she was *free*.

Caught somewhere *between* wanting to live in a city loft sipping cocktails in stilettos, and living on a ranch, next to a carefree campfire, holding a guitar, and shotgunning a beer.

Ever see *that car* with their signal on,
waiting for someone to let them into busy traffic,
not making any effort, because they are too meek
and scared to merge…
Never be *that* car.
Take charge.
Move in.
Speed.
Get what you want.
No excuses.
Drive.

Life is far too beautiful to live it broken.

Success comes from making all *your* grey areas into black borders.

Don't you dare hide her -
She's meant to shine, to glisten, to glow.

There is a reason why when an airplane goes down you are told to put the oxygen mask on yourself first, before anyone else, even before a loved one. It's not because of selfishness, or lack of altruism, it's because if you can't help yourself, give yourself the oxygen you need, you can never properly help others around you, you are of no use. *Self care* and *self love* are needed in order for *you* to help, protect and care for those that *you* love. ***Give yourself oxygen when it is needed.***

He changed her,
for the rest of
her life,
but it's up
to her to decide,
if that's a bad
or a good thing.

*Anger* can kill you.
It first starts in the mind,
eats away at the soul,
then your body reacts to the repercussions.
Let go, forgive, take credit for mistakes,
move on and release.
Tell those that matter,
you care and always will.
Do it for them, do it for *you*.
Don't be a victim to your own inability to
rationally make a decision to free yourself from your mind.
You are worth more than that.
*Your life* is precious.

Always a she-wolf.

Beautiful girl,
remember,
*self-respect* comes first.

Be that girl who knows
she can make it entirely on her own,
but also;
be that girl who knows life is more
beautiful when you share it.

Honey,
you are just in your opening act -
wait till you see the finale.

A hopeless romantic
with a dirty mind,
a taste for tequila
and a necessary air kick
whenever her
favourite song plays.

She had dreams,
like performing in front of a New York audience,
like having her love in the crowd cheering her on.
She still has dreams,
but the second part will no longer happen with *that* love.

Yes you indeed
have *made mistakes*,
but understand
*your mistakes*
don't make you.

And she'll take funny over looks,
honesty over status,
ridiculous over boring,
and character over money,
every time.
Every. Time.

*Make her crawl*
and she'll start to enjoy the ground
so much,
that she'll make friends with the
insects,
build a home on the waterfront of the
biggest gaping puddle,
and bask in the sun covered in soot.
*She'll find the best in her circumstances.*
Regardless if it's a mansion on the cliff
of the highest mountain,
or the *slums of hell.*
Take away every item,
every possession,
but you can't take away
*her mental strength.*
She'll fall in love with life,
any which way,
over and over and over again.
So go ahead,
*please,*
make her crawl.

Things don't always come back around.
Sometimes they end with *almost*.
Sometimes *almost* is *the end*.

Not the damsel.
Not in distress.
She's the one in the shiny metal armour,
fighting the dragons,
reclaiming her
throne.

"Tread lightly," they say to her, "hearts break in the blink of an eye."
*She blinked her eyes.* "Nothing happened," she replied.
With a half smirk on her face she continued,
"what you don't know, is that this heart is *already* broken"

She collects moments, memories,
and midnight kisses,
while other people spend their time
collecting things.

It's a beautiful thing
when you get
to that point
where
instead of
fearing change
you welcome
and embrace it.

With age
should come
wisdom;
Anger, hostility
and a temper
will get
you nowhere.
With age you become
wise with
your emotions,
compassionate
with your thoughts,
and mindful
with your time.

She wanted that magical love story,
or she wanted nothing at all.

Heart of hearts, they see
she's the kind of girl
that could
break up a band;
the kind of girl,
that could bring
one back together.

Be it career,
heartbreak,
starting over,
or accomplishing goals,
one of the best feelings
in the world
is to look back
and see
how far
you have come.

If you don't
listen to
what all the sheep say,
you can be a collaboration of
everything they said
*you could never be.*

Be a river. Keep on going, in one direction – never look back.

Let that wound heal, you owe it to yourself.

Ladies,
what matters most is what lies inside a man's heart;
none of us die and get to take the handbags with us.

As she turned the corner
walking away
into the unknown galaxies
beyond this world,
he uttered, "I love you",
under his breath.
She didn't hear him,
nor did he want her to.
He knew if she did,
even *that* wouldn't be enough
to make her stay.

He broke her,
she healed herself.
He lost her,
and he never saw her again.
The end.

Don't forget,
failure is also
a fresh start.

Use a blanket
Use water
Use an extinguisher
But never use your arms
to put out
someone else's fire.

And oh, how he hoped all the names and games he played would have crushed her, for her to never open her heart to someone new. And oh, how he was so very wrong.

Welcome back,
grab a seat,
because you are here
for the long haul.
not in passing.
It's okay,
for a moment,
you got lost
and forgot
*who you are.*
So, welcome back
and let's see
where this
new road
takes you.

Part 4

# I Guess I Wrote Some Love Poems

It's the sideways look
sitting next to each other
watching a performance
looking over at her
and thinks she doesn't notice
and she notices
smiles inside
but pretends
she doesn't see.

When she was in 8th grade,
and he moved to her school,
he sat behind her in English class.
He peered over her shoulder and watched,
as she wrote her full name with an HB Pencil.
Then he tapped on her shoulder, and said,
"What a name."
She turned abruptly and looked back at this
new stranger and ignored him.
But he continued, and said,
"I'm going to make you change it."
She turned back again and gave him a dirty look.
She felt teased and asked the teacher
if she could move seats,
so she did.
But years later,
as she looks at him,
on this day
down that aisle,
walking towards him,
in her *wedding dress*,
she finally understands,
what he *actually meant*.

He could tame her ferociousness,
and that is what made him *different*.

And when their eyes met,
there was something *nostalgic*.
Like they were old souls that met again.
Maybe it was the warm summer night,
or the full smiles and happy champagne glasses,
but whatever it was,
*it was real.*
Because in that moment,
two complete strangers,
for the first time in their lives,
understood
*soul mates* do exist.

Being lost with him is always okay.

She might have layers,
but he plans on ripping them all off.

Somewhere in the middle of Houston
on a boring Tuesday,
a man pulled up to a girl
in a red Mustang, singing
out of tune with the music in
both their cars,
and from that moment on,
he knew –
she was
the one.

If you find the
beauty in pain,
it can make all
the difference.

For such a man,
when he laughs
he laughs with his
head tilted back
like a little kid
without a care
in the world,
And every time
he does,
it makes her
smile without
one either.

One single rose
One single kiss
One single laugh
One single grab

…and she was no
longer single.

He was interesting,
and out of all of his qualities
being a dapper handsome man,
was his least interesting.

There was *you*
There was *me*
Eyes from *you*
Looked at *me*
In that moment
Clear to see
There was no *you*
There was no *me*
And only *us*
We would now be

She just wanted love –
that real, passionate,
rip her clothes off on a Tuesday as soon as you get home from work
kind of love.

And with one look, one quirky smile, one ounce of nervousness,
she blushed for the first time
in *a long time.*

What a breath of fresh air he is.

And I would happily get lost trying to find you,
over and over again.

You are enchantingly weird.
I like you.

"Take the chance," the heart said,
"if I get broken again, I'll find a way to get fixed again."

The End

# About the Author

Shana Marlayna Chow is a certified life coach and author. She holds a Bachelor of Arts in Social Sciences from Simon Fraser University, and a Life Coach Certification through Rhodes Wellness College. Shana is a creative soul, has a background in acting, and writes music lyrics as well as fiction.

This is Shana's second book of poetry, following *Love Gone Savage*, a poetic exploration of the mind, released in 2017.

*I Tried to Write Love Poems* is a journey anyone going through a heartbreak can relate to. Follow through the emotional roller coaster of the 4 stages of a break up, while learning the lesson that letting go takes time, but overall happiness is dependent on healing and being patient with the process.

If you'd like to get in touch with Shana, or learn more about her life coaching packages, visit her website at www.shanachow.com, or follow her writing account on instagram @shanamchow

CPSIA information can be obtained
at www.ICGtesting.com
Printed in the USA
LVHW080230201219
641200LV00013B/143/P

9 781999 273705